CHROMEBOOK

FOR BEGINNERS

A Comprehensive Guide for Beginners and Seniors to
Master The New Chromebook Like A Pro

GW00454904

Todd A. Holmes

i

Contents

Introduction

Chrome, Google's market-leading web browser, has evolved into an operating system that is only available on Chromebooks, Google-powered computers. These low-cost Chrome OS laptops are cloud-based deals that can help anyone get work done for a fraction of the price of a MacBook or Windows laptop. Chromebooks have come a long way since their debut in 2011. Chromebooks are worth a second look if your company needs quickly deployable, adaptable, and secure laptops to provide to staff, especially if you haven't used one in a while.

The cheat sheet on Chromebooks from Tec Republic is both a fast introduction to these laptops and a "live" document that will be updated when new models and features are available. Chromebooks are laptops that run the Google-licensed Chrome OS, which is built on the Linux kernel. Chrome OS is incredibly minimal, relying nearly entirely on the Chrome browser for its user interface. Chromebooks are made by a number of different companies, including Google, HP, Acer, Samsung, Dell, and others.

Why are Chromebooks so important?

Chrome OS and the hardware that run it are both extremely light. Those computers are simple to update, wipe with little effort, and are cheap enough to be readily replaced. Chromebooks are popular in schools and businesses because they are low-maintenance gadgets. G Suite users may get even more out of Chromebooks because the integration is simple and users log in with the same Google account they use at work. Because many of these devices now run Android apps capable of exchanging data between both devices, Chromebooks make working on an Android device and a laptop more practical.

What features do Chromebooks provide for businesses, and how do they compare to the iPad?

In overall sales, Chromebooks surpassed MacBooks in 2016, signifying a shift in computing priorities: the cloud reigns supreme, and the machine is merely a terminal. If you only use your work laptop for word processing, responding to emails, working with spreadsheets, and other basic office duties, there's no reason to spend $2,000 on a MacBook when you can accomplish the same things for a fraction of the price on a Chromebook.

The following are some of the aspects that business users interested in Chromebooks should be aware of:

- Users are prevented from forgetting to install security updates through automatic updating.
- User information is encrypted and cannot be accessed by other users on the device.

- Chromebook processes are all sandboxed, so compromising one won't give you access to another; and Read-only code verifies bootup by checking writable code for harmful modifications. Apple's new iPad is positioned as a direct competitor to Chromebooks, raising the dilemma of which one to buy. Chromebooks are the most cost-effective option: Cheap ones cost approximately $300, although Apple's new 9.7-inch iPad, which is being marketed as a Chromebook rival, starts at $329 without a keyboard.

If you're debating whether to get a Chromebook or an iPad with a keyboard, keep in mind the ecosystem: if you already use Android and other Google products, you'll get more use out of a Chromebook, whereas if you're invested in Apple products like Macs and iOS devices, the iPad is probably the better choice. If you prefer a tablet, detachable Chromebooks like the HP Chromebook x2 can be used in the same way as a keyboard-less iPad, though at a somewhat higher price of $600 against $329 for the iPad. Chromebooks have a security advantage over regular laptops and even iOS devices. Chromebooks are extremely safe; see The Chromium Project's list of Chrome OS security features for more information. In October 2019, HP unveiled a new line of enterprise-focused Chromebooks and other Chrome OS devices, similar to Dell's Latitude Chromebooks, which were released earlier in the year. Chromebooks are becoming more enterprise-friendly, and it won't be long before the trend spreads, especially as more and more work (and enjoyment) is done utilizing web services rather to locally installed software on a desktop or laptop.

Chapter 1

Getting Started with Chromebook

Choosing and Setting Up Your Chromebook

If you've been following technology news recently, you've definitely heard about Google's Chromebook, which is making yet another splash in the hardware industry. In 2013, they accounted for 1% of the laptop market in the United States, equating to around 2.5 million units sold, a figure that is likely to rise. In this chapter, I discuss what distinguishes the Chromebook from other personal laptops on the market. I also go over how to set up your Chromebook in detail and how to make the switch from Windows or Mac to Chromebook. Setting up your Chromebook is a three-step process, and that's only if "turn it on" is included. Ready? Here's how to do it:

1. Switch it on.
2. Sign into your Google account after selecting your language and connecting to your Wi-Fi network.
3. Select a profile photo or icon (I'd prefer an icon, but I'm bashful).

That's all there is to it: you're done. After there, using a Chromebook is simply a matter of gathering the apps you require. Calendar, Google Drive, the full suite of Google Docs tools, YouTube, Google Meet, and Chrome remote desktop are already included. Any other apps can be found in the Chrome Web Store. You can add new users to your Chromebook from the login page if you're sharing it with others in your household. Simply have them connect in with their Google account in the same way you did. When friends come over and need to check their email, you can give them the opportunity to log in as guests. There is no preparation required for guests; simply select "Login as guest" from the login screen. Oh, and you may have heard that Chromebooks can only function if they are connected to the internet. That's not quite true; many Chrome apps, including Gmail Offline, Google Drawings, and even Android Apps from Google Play, offer an offline mode as well—though you should proceed with caution, as mobile apps don't always work well on the desktop.

Understanding the inner workings of a Chromebook

Keys on your Chromebook keyboard that aren't found anywhere else. From left to right, your Chromebook keys are normally found on the top row of your keyboard. or to search, show your apps, and interact with Google Assistant, press the Search or Launcher keys. Press Alt + Search to enable or disable Caps Lock. Alternately, press Alt + Launcher. Back to previous page Continue to the next page. Reload the current page Make your page fill the entire screen. Display all of your open windows. Take a picture of it. Reduce the screen's brightness. Increase the brightness of the screen Set the electronic privacy screen to on. Reduce the brightness of the keyboard backlight. Increase the brightness of the keyboard lighting. Return to the previous track. Play/pause Toggle to the next track Turn off the music. Reduce the volume. Turn up the volume.

Repair any issues with your keyboard.

You may be at the top or lower limit for that setting if the volume or brightness keys don't work. If the past and forward buttons don't work, see if the identical icons are grayed out in a web browser window. If the back button on a webpage is gray, for example, the browser is unaware of a page to which it might return.

If you're having further issues with your keyboard, try the following:

Turn the Chromebook off and then on again.

While browsing as a guest, use the keys. If the keys work, delete the account on your Chromebook that is causing the issue and then re-add it. Perform a hard reset on the hardware of your Chromebook.

Perform a factory reset on the Chromebook if the owner account is having issues.

If you're still having problems after attempting these instructions, contact the manufacturer of your Chromebook.

Make better use of your keyboard.

- Take advantage of keyboard shortcuts.
- Change the language on your keyboard.
- Change the default search engine for the Search key.
- Use the keyboard that appears on the screen.
- Configure your Chromebook

- You'll need the following items to set up your Chromebook or Chromebox:
- Username and password for your Google Account
- A network connection is required.
- Turn on your Chromebook first.
- Install the battery if it's been removed.
- To turn it on, press the power button.

Follow the directions on the screen.

Select the language that displays on the screen to select your language and keyboard settings.

- Select Accessibility to enable accessibility features.
- Select a network to join.
- Accept the terms and conditions of service.

Use your Google Account to log in.

Enter your Google Account email or phone number, as well as your password, to select the owner of your Chromebook.

- If you've enabled 2-Step Verification, you'll get a code on your chosen device.
- Create a Google Account if you don't already have one. You can choose More choices on various Chromebooks. Make a new account.
- Select Browse as Guest to use your Chromebook without creating an account.

Use the sign-in troubleshooter if you're experiencing problems signing in with your Google Account. Your bookmarks, extensions, and apps will show automatically after you sign in.

For the first time, you're using your Chromebook.

Chromebooks, on the other hand, have a steep learning curve and a distinct feel than, say, a MacBook or a Surface Laptop. You might also be unsure what a Chromebook can accomplish or how to set it up.

Here are the greatest Chromebook tips and techniques for new owners.

1. **Create a number of different user profiles.**

Chromebooks make extensive use of Chrome's User Profiles feature, which allows you to divide your system into multiple login profiles. Each profile has its own collection of apps, preferences, and controls. Are you the only one who uses your computer? Using numerous profiles is still a good idea. If you have children, though, Chromebook user profiles are essential. Google discontinued monitored profiles in favor of the Google Family Link, which is fairly comparable. To create secure accounts for your children, follow Christian's instructions for installing Google Family Link on Android. For a Chromebook, the procedure is the same.

2. **For visitors, use Guest Mode.**

Even if you don't use the above-mentioned Profiles option, you should be aware of Guest Mode. Guest Mode allows you to give your device to someone else and know that they won't be able to see or use your data (e.g., browsing history, downloads, bookmarks, etc.). When the guest leaves, all traces of their presence are erased from your device, eliminating the need for manual housekeeping. While this may appear to be similar to Chrome's Incognito Mode, be warned that the two are not the same!

3. Open each app in its own window

Locate the appropriate app in the App Launcher or Taskbar, right-click it, and choose Open as window from the menu that appears. That's all there is to it! Your gadget will no longer feel like a glorified Chrome browser, but rather a full-fledged laptop.

4. Separate your apps into folders.

You'll soon have too many installed apps to keep track of as you use your cellphone more and more. While the Program Launcher makes it simple to search for and start any app, you may prefer to tap or click. In that situation, App Folders should come in handy. To create a folder, open the App Launcher and select All Apps, then drag any program icon onto any other app icon. Continue dragging as many symbols as you need. To rename the folder, right-click it and change "Unnamed Folder" to whatever you want at the top.

REASONS TO USE A CHROMEBOOK INSTEAD OF A WINDOWS COMPUTER

5. Converting Websites to Apps

Keep in mind that Chromebook apps are just websites disguised as apps. While there are some drawbacks, there is one very useful feature: you can transform any website into an app and run it in its own window. Open Chrome, go to the website you wish to use as an app, and then click the three-dot icon in the top right corner. Select Create shortcut from the More tools menu. Give the program a name, check the Open as window box, and click Add.

6. Before you open a file, take a look at it first.

One of the nicest features of macOS Finder is that you can highlight almost any file and press Spacebar to receive a preview of it without having to open it in its associated program. Did you know that Chrome OS includes a preview feature as well? Open the Files app and hit Spacebar to select any file without actually opening it. An overlay will appear showing file details (e.g., size, type, last changed time, and so on) as well as information unique to the file type (e.g., ID3 tags for MP3s). A preview will be available for some categories, such as photographs and audio.

7. Align the windows to the left and right of the screen.

You probably don't want to maximize your apps if you have a Chromebook with a resolution of 1920x1080 or above. You may make greater use of your screen real estate by keeping two windows open side by side for increased productivity. Drag windows to the left or right edge of the screen, and Chrome OS will automatically snap them to the side and fill half of the screen. You may also choose a window and press Alt + [to snap it to the left or Alt +] to snap it to the right.

8. For Frozen Apps, Force Quit

On Chrome OS, you're less likely to encounter frozen programs than on Windows or even Mac. If you do, all you have to do is use the Search button + Escape keyboard shortcut to access the Task Manager. Simply find the frozen process, pick it, and click End Process once it's opened. One of the most significant Chrome OS features is the Task Manager, so make sure you start utilizing it right away.

9. For a Frozen System, Force a Reboot

In the unlikely event that something goes wrong at the system level, the Task Manager may not open or be able to unfreeze your device. If this happens, you can always perform a hard reboot as a final resort. Above the number key row on every Chromebook is a specific set of media keys. The Refresh key (which looks like a circular arrow) is one of them, while the Power key is another (looks like a circle with a vertical line). To restart your computer right away, press Power + Refresh. **Note** that any unsaved data in open apps will be lost. It's also worth noting that this isn't the same as a Power wash, which is discussed in greater depth further down.

10. Learn how to use the built-in search function.

Chromebook keyboards are notable for their lack of a Windows or Command key. Instead, Google replaced the Caps Lock key with a Search key that, when touched, launches the App Launcher.

This key is beneficial in three ways:

Type the name of any app to quickly launch it. In this way, it's analogous to the Start Menu in Windows 10 and Spotlight in Mac OS X.

- Launch any website URL or search engine query in a flash.
- By pressing the microphone button, you can start a voice search.

It may seem strange to utilize the Caps Lock key in this manner, but once you get into the swing of it, going back is impossible.

- Rebind the Special Keys to their original positions.
11.   Five keys are treated as special in Chrome OS, and you can remind them if you want: Search, Ctrl, Alt, Backspace, and

Escape. These, as well as Caps Lock, Google Assistant, and Disabled, can be reminded to any of the other five keys. Do you despise the Search key? Here, set it to Caps Lock. Alternatively, turn it off completely.

To open Settings, click your profile symbol in the bottom right corner, then the gear icon. Select Device > Keyboard from the drop-down menu. Simply use the drop-down menus to change the key bindings. By checking the box, you can also convert the top-row media keys to function keys.

12.   Become familiar with the system's keyboard shortcuts

Chromebooks use various keyboard shortcuts for system-level actions in addition to having a different keyboard layout. Fortunately, Google made learning these new shortcuts relatively simple by incorporating another shortcut into the process. The Chromebook shortcut dictionary can be accessed by pressing **CTRL + ALT +?** (yep, the question mark key). To find the shortcut you desire, type in a letter. You can use the dictionary to look up a shortcut for a single letter or key, or to see which Chromebook shortcuts use a given combination. Starting with the most common alternatives, it lists every potential Chromebook shortcut. However, you can get a head start by reviewing our list of the most useful Chromebook shortcuts.

13.   Touchpad Right-Click and Middle-Click

My first three days on my Chromebook were miserable because the touchpad lacked any mouse buttons. Because I didn't have access to right-clicking or middle-clicking, web browsing became a nightmare. Both of these actions turn out to be much easier than I had anticipated. To right-click, simply tap the touchpad with two fingers at the same time. To middle-click, simply tap the touchpad with three fingers at the same time. Simply following this suggestion can vastly improve your Chromebook experience.

14.   Swipe Gestures for the Touchpad

Modern Chromebooks include a gesture-enabled touchpad, and these movements will revolutionize your life. While many gestures are supported, every Chromebook beginner should be aware of the following four:

- To go forward and back in Chrome, swipe horizontally with two fingers.
- To scroll up and down, swipe vertically with two fingers.
- To switch between open tabs in Chrome, swipe horizontally with three fingers. Ctrl + Tab is faster, but this is even faster.
- To open the Task Switcher, swipe down with three fingers, which spreads out all open apps in a bird's eye perspective.

15.   Make   Disk   Space   Available Immediately

All Chromebooks include a solid-state drive (SSD) for data storage. While this is excellent news in terms of speed and performance, there is one drawback: many Chromebooks have relatively little SSDs. On one hand, this is advantageous because it lowers the cost of a new Chromebook. On the other hand, you might quickly run out of storage capacity. That's why disk space management is crucial. To open Settings, click your profile symbol in the bottom right corner, then the gear icon. Click Storage management under the Device section. You can check what's taking up space on your machine and erase it with a single click if necessary.

You may replace the SSD in some Chromebooks with a bigger capacity one. If you replace the SSD, your warranty may be voided, so double-check before making any hardware changes. If you'd rather not mess with the hardware, look into the lowest cloud storage options.

16.   Turn off the Sleep Mode

For a long time, Chrome OS didn't provide users with a good way to regulate screen idle time and battery consumption. That is, thankfully, no longer the case. You can choose what your Chromebook should do when it is idle by going to Settings > Power. For reference, after about 10-minutes, your Chromebook will begin to idle. You can choose to go to sleep, turn off the display, or keep it on. Many people prefer the latter option because returning to a sleeping Chromebook is inconvenient. You may also turn off Sleep while the lid is closed, which prevents your device from napping every time you close the lid.

Due to school or company administrative settings, some individuals may be unable to access such options. If that describes you, try disabling Sleep Mode with this Chrome extension. Furthermore, the Keep Awake extension allows you to choose between screen-only and screen-and-system sleep modes.

17.   Take Screenshots with Ease

How are you expected to capture an image of your screen if your Chromebook doesn't have a Print Screen button? Simply hold down the Ctrl key while pressing the Switch Window key. (The top-row key Switch Window is shaped like a rectangle with two vertical lines beside it.) Saved screenshots are stored in your Downloads folder, which can be accessed through the Files app. You may also use **Ctrl + Shift +** Switch Window to limit your screenshot to a specified area of the screen by pressing **Ctrl + Shift +** Switch Window.

18. Use Flags to Enable Optional Features

To access a variety of optional Chrome OS features, open Chrome and type chrome:/flags in the URL bar. Please keep in mind that some of these optional features may not be totally stable. They may, at best, not operate as planned. They may be buggy enough to cause data loss in the worst-case scenario. Although the most of them are near-stable, and severe issues are uncommon, this danger is always present with these optional features.

19. Beta and Dev Channels Have Experimental Features

Consider moving to the Beta or Dev channel if you're feeling adventurous but don't want to fiddle with the optional flags above. The Beta channel allows you to get a low-risk sneak peek at planned features around a month before the Stable channel. The Dev channel gives you a high-risk, bug-prone preview of experimental features before the Stable channel.

To change to the Beta or Dev channels, follow these steps:

- At the lower right, click your profile symbol.
- To open Settings, click the gear symbol.
- Click About Chrome OS at the bottom of the left window.
- Select Additional Details from the drop-down menu.
- Change the channel by pressing the Change channel button.
- Choose between the Beta and Dev channels.

Stick to the Stable channel if you wish to reduce system crashes and the risk of data loss. Switching from an experimental to a stable channel will wipe your Chromebook clean, including your accounts!

20.   Using Power wash to Reset the Factory

You may need to Powerwash your device if you ever wish to start over with a clean slate, intend on selling your Chromebook, or if you ever run into a catastrophic mistake that causes your system to fail all the time. A "factory reset" is referred to as a "powerwash" by Google. It wipes your Chromebook clean of all data and resets it to factory settings. Despite the loss of local data, your Google accounts and profiles, as well as any data synchronized to Google's cloud, will be unaffected.

21.   Enable Google Assistant.

On your Chromebook, you may utilize the Google Assistant to display notifications, "OK Google," and other valuable information. Google Assistant can assist new Chromebook users in navigating the device. It shows you useful tooltips and other information related to your current activity. To activate Google Assistant, go to the bottom right corner of your screen and click your profile symbol, then the gear icon to open Settings. Go to Google Assistant > Search and Assistant.

Chromebooks, like other computers, slow down over time as a result of wear and tear and the collection of garbage, albeit you're unlikely to require an antivirus on one. Fortunately, there are things you may take to improve the performance of your Chromebook. Check out the top Chromebooks for every sort of user if you're looking for a change of pace with your Chromebook. Last but not least, even though I shout their praises and believe Chromebooks are the finest gadget for casual home usage, they aren't flawless. Here's how to install Linux on your Chromebook if you want to try something new.

Switching from a Windows or Mac computer to a Chromebook

- **Open your Chrome browser and log in.**

Grab your old Mac/Windows machine and make sure your Chrome browser is signed in with your Google account. All of your bookmarks, passwords, and settings will be kept for the switch if you do it this way.

- **Ensure that your stuff is secure.**

Documents, photographs, and videos

Download Drive for desktop and sign in with your Google account to back up your data, photographs, and videos easily and safely. Then, depending on whether you want to upload to Drive, Photos, or both, select the folders and devices you wish to upload. You'll be able to import your Apple Photos Library into Google

Photos as well. You can back up your work to an external hard drive and connect it to your Chromebook later if you don't want to download Drive for desktop.

- **Log in to your new Chromebook for the first time.**

Check that you're using the same Google account as in Steps 1 and 2. When you open Google Drive, you should see all of your files waiting for you. Connect your external hard drive to your Chromebook if you used one. Download the YouTube Music app or launch Apple Music and sign in with your Apple ID to begin listening to your music.

Chapter 2

Utilizing the Desktop

The Chromebook desktop is a visual interface that controls, organizes, and manages files, data, and programs using a windowing system. You can use a mouse, keyboard, touch screen, or your voice to interact. Finally, there is a launch point on your desktop where you can manually traverse your computer's file system. The Start button or the taskbar are used by Microsoft Windows, and the dock is used by Macintosh. This launching point on your Chromebook is known as the shelf.

Finding your way around the Chromebook shelf

Getting Around on the Chrome OS Desktop

Chrome OS has a desktop interface that resembles Windows or Mac OS in appearance and feel. You can make many windows appear on your desktop, and you can size and organize them however you want.

Look through the shelves

The Shelf, which is similar to the taskbar in Windows, runs along the bottom border of the desktop. This section offers icons for your most frequently used programs. The Launcher, Google Chrome, Gmail, Google Docs, YouTube, and the Google Play Store are all default icons on the Shelf; you may also pin more apps to it. To open an app in a new window, click its icon.

Activate the App Drawer

The Launcher is the first icon on the Shelf. The App Drawer, which is similar to Chrome's version of the Windows Start menu, is accessed through the Launcher. Select the Launcher icon from the menu bar (or, on a touchscreen display, use your finger to drag the Shelf up).

The initial App Drawer panel is visible. This panel has a search bar where you may look for programs and files on your Chromebook, as well as icons for the apps you've recently used. To reopen an app, simply click it. To make the App Drawer occupy the entire screen, click the up arrow at the top of the App Drawer (or drag up the top of the App Drawer on a touchscreen display).

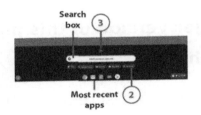

To see a larger version of this photograph, please click here.

The App Drawer's full-screen version gives you access to all of the programs on your

Chromebook. To open an app, simply click on its icon. The full-screen App Drawer takes up numerous pages if you have a lot of apps loaded. To access another page of apps, click one of the round icons on the right side of the screen. (Or use your finger to scroll from one page to the next on a touchscreen Chromebook.) Click the Launcher icon again to close either version of the App Drawer.

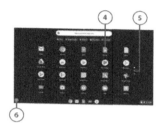

To see a larger version of this photograph, please click here.

The App Drawer's full-screen version gives you access to all of the programs on your Chromebook. To open an app, simply click on its icon. The full-screen App Drawer takes up numerous pages if you have a lot of apps loaded. To access another page of apps, click one of the round icons on the right side of the screen. (Or use your finger to scroll from one page to the next on a touchscreen Chromebook.)

Click the Launcher icon again to close either version of the App Drawer.

To see a larger version of this photograph, please click here.

- Drag an icon and drop it on top of another to make a new folder.

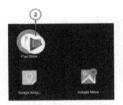

- The newly created folder now contains both icons. To open that folder, simply click on it.

Simply drag another icon onto the folder icon or into the open folder to add it to the folder. In the Unnamed field, type a name for the folder. To get rid of an icon from a folder, open it and drag it out.

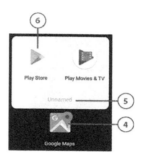

Look at the System Tray

The System Tray is located on the far right side of the Shelf. The System Tray contains system information as well as access to your own settings.

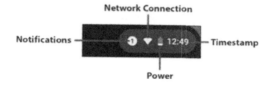

Notifications, Network Connection (Wi-Fi), Power (battery level or AC), and Timestamp (date and time) are the four basic status symbols in the status section, though you may see different icons depending on the situation. Use the Quick Settings Panel to customize your settings. The Quick Settings panel, which you reach from the System Tray, may be used to customize several of the most regularly used Chrome system settings. The Quick Settings window will appear when you click anywhere on the System Tray.

- The top of the Quick Settings panel displays notifications. To proceed to the next notice, click or swipe it (on a touchscreen display).
- To switch off your Chromebook, go to Settings > Power.
- To secure your Chromebook, click Lock.
- To open the Settings window, click Settings. From there, you can change other system settings.

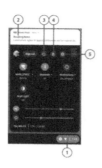

Settings for the Chromebook Operating System

"Configuring and Personalizing Chrome OS," you'll learn more about configuring Chrome OS settings. To view and switch to other Wi-Fi networks, go to Wi-Fi. Toggle on or off Bluetooth wireless communication by clicking Bluetooth. To customize notification settings, go to Notifications. Toggle the Night Light mode on or off by clicking the button. To adjust the volume on your Chromebook, drag the Volume slider up or down. Increase or reduce screen brightness by dragging the Brightness slider. Hide the Quick Settings panel by clicking the down arrow.

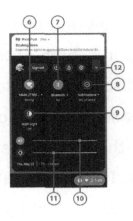

Organizing and adding apps

It can be very daunting at times if you enjoy installing and testing out new apps on your Android smartphone. Whether you have a lot or a few apps, everyone can benefit from some assistance in keeping their Android apps organized.

Here are five creative and innovative ways to keep your app drawer clean, organised, and beautiful, ranging from managing apps to renaming folders.

1. Make a list of your apps based on what they do.

Don't waste time browsing through your phone's default app names in search of the one you need. Instead, make a list of your folders and rename them with verb-based descriptions that describe what you do with them, such as "watch," "play," "learn," and so on. It will only take a few seconds to locate an app when you need to return to it. If your phone allows it, you can do this on your home screen or in your app drawer. Just make sure to label each app with the correct verb. For example, for a folder holding clipboard manager software, "Copy" is an excellent choice. For pedometer or workout apps that chart your daily walk pattern, "Walks" is a preferable moniker. On your Android device, you may organize several apps into a folder and give it a name.

2. Use Shortcuts and Widgets to Easily Access Apps

Thankfully, Android provides a plethora of options for getting the most out of your phone. You can use shortcuts or widgets to position frequently-used apps on the edge of your home screen for quick access when switching between programs. How you hold and utilize your device determines a lot. You can, for example, put an email app on the left side of your screen and a phone app on the right, or wherever you choose. It merely takes one swipe to open the app you require from there. Samsung's devices make this a lot easier thanks to an innovative edge panel design that allows you to quickly swipe between your apps.

3. Make an alphabetical list

A straightforward, methodical, and efficient folder structure is achieved by categorizing your apps in alphabetical order. There are two methods for organizing your apps in this way. You can use the default app sort option on various devices, including those from Samsung, as seen below:

- Tap the three-dot menu in the top-right corner to open the Apps screen.
- Select Display layout > Alphabetical order from the drop-down menu. You can also go

to Menu > Sort > Alphabetical order or Arrange by A to Z on some smartphones, or something similar.

The apps in your library should now be organized alphabetically. Alternatively, you can establish a "A" Folder and a "B" Folder, and sort all the programs with names that begin with A, B, and so on into those folders.

4. Increase the number of home screens

In order of how frequently you utilize your apps, try adding extra home screen pages. Start by pinning your most-used apps to your Android device's main screen, such as your browser, email, or phone app. It's simple to add a new home screen page. While the steps may vary by device, here's a general overview of how it works on most phones: Start by long-pressing an app to add it to your Home screen. Drag it to the right edge of your Android home screen, then hit the + sign. Release to move the icon or widget to the new home screen's desired location. You can organize and place apps on the second and third pages of your screen, and so on, as you add more to your phone. Apps that don't need to be checked as regularly, such as weather or navigation apps, or gaming apps, can be placed on the second and third displays. You should also choose an ideal grid size for app distribution, such as "4 x 5" or another, so that you can view and manage your apps more easily.

5. Use Emojis to Name Folders

The same-old titles for folders like "Games" and "Music" can get a little tedious. Add an emoji label to each folder, or a mix of text and emojis, to make them stand out. The music symbol, for example, can be used to indicate a folder holding programs such as SoundCloud and Spotify. Giving an app a descriptive emoji name makes it easier than ever to find when you're looking for it. This is how you do it.

Create a new folder for your selected programs.

In the Folder name field, tap the default emoji keyboard and type your favorite emoji(s). Text inputs can also be used in conjunction with emojis. After that, simply tap anywhere on the screen to create a new folder.

Make a list of your apps based on their function or purpose.

Organizing your apps by context can make it easier to find what you're looking for. Create different folders for different functions, such as calendar management, social media, and note-taking, and place the appropriate apps in each one. You could want to organize your apps into groups based on how they're used. Create a folder titled "Work" for example, if you want to put all of your work-related apps in one spot. Personal communications, health and fitness, and gaming applications can all be categorized as "Personal."

Make use of a color-coded folder system.

This is a more natural and easier method to arrange your smartphone apps, using a unique blend of color and images. Simply group your apps into folders based on their icon colors. It might make your entire smartphone experience a little more enjoyable, and it might even give your app screen that rainbow-themed liveliness. It might not work for everyone, especially if you want to categorize apps based on their functionality.

Store infrequently-

Apps that have been used in the past are kept in a separate folder. Apps might be useful, but let's face it: you probably don't use half of the ones you have. Use this clever little hack to save space in your storage. Apps that you infrequently use can be moved to a "Old" folder for future reference. Your home screen will be less cluttered as a result of this. If you have a Samsung phone, you should take use of some of the company's unique customization choices for organizing and managing apps, such as the "Zipped apps" function, which allows you to disable and store less-used programs in a different folder.

Transfer your apps to a microSD card

If your smartphone doesn't come with enough storage or you're attempting to save space on your phone, installing too many apps can cause complications. Fortunately, you can always transfer resource-intensive programs to a microSD card in a few easy steps:

- Navigate to Settings > Apps on your device.
- Choose the app you want to save to your microSD card.
- If necessary, go to Storage > Change (if applicable) > Move.

This function isn't available on all devices. The apps cannot be transferred if the Change option is not available.

Take advantage of app launchers

Launchers are used to enhance the usefulness of smartphones by allowing you to access all of your Android's capabilities, such as controlling apps in new ways, changing default user interface themes, and customizing icons and widgets for convenience and customization. App launchers can help you manage your app drawer and customize your home screen in a variety of ways.

Increase the Power of Your Android Experience

Getting your app drawer organized can make a big difference. It may take some time to set everything up, but once you've done so, you'll never have to waste time looking for that particular program again. Organize your apps to speed up your mobile device. Ensure that you never waste time looking through a cluttered app drawer, maximizing the performance, experience, and usability of your phone.

Changing Chromebook preferences

Chromebooks make it simple to personalize the look and feel of your computer. While there aren't as many customization options as there are in Windows or macOS, you can still customize your desktop wallpaper and browser theme.

To change your background, follow these steps:

The wallpaper on your desktop is the first thing you see when you sign in to your Chromebook, so make sure you like it.

- In the bottom-right corner, click the status tray.
- From the pop-up menu, choose Settings.
- Select Wallpaper from the Personalization menu in the Settings menu.

There will be a menu with a variety of wallpapers to choose from. Choose the wallpaper you wish to use as your background by clicking on it.

The wallpaper on your desktop will be changed.

- To change the theme of your browser, go to:

You'll be using the Chrome browser a lot because Chromebooks are mostly based on it. The default look, on the other hand, can grow a little monotonous after a while. Fortunately, you can modify the look of your browser by selecting from a variety of themes. In the bottom-left corner, click the launcher symbol. Then, in the search field, type browser themes.

- Select Chrome Web Store from the drop-down menu.

In the Chrome Web Store, a Themes window will display. Choose the theme you'd want to use. A web page with more information about the theme appears. To install the theme, go to Chrome > Add to Chrome. Your browser will be updated with the theme.

Understanding Chromebook window controls

If you don't require a laptop that can handle demanding programs, Chromebooks are fantastic. Getting a Chromebook is a fantastic option if you're only interested in the browser experience. Some aspects, though, can become excessive. A good example is the touchscreen. It's fine for casual browsing and provides a good mix of smartphone and laptop navigation. However, you'll want to turn off your Chromebook's touchscreen and touchpad from time to time. Fortunately, Google has thought of everything and made turning on/off the touch screen a breeze.

Why Is the Touchscreen Disabled?

A touchscreen on a laptop is fantastic. You can use the screen without having to use the touchpad while still typing on the keyboard. However, there will be instances when you just want to point at the screen and nothing will happen. This is why Google has made it possible to turn it on and off at any time. Let's say you choose to utilize the touchscreen instead of the touchpad. Perhaps you've connected your standard mouse to your

Chromebook. Occasionally, you'll accidently touch the touchpad while typing, causing the pointer to move annoyingly. Worse, you might accidentally click and commit an activity you didn't intend to undertake. This is why Chromebooks include a simple way to turn on or off the touchpad.

Disabling the Touchpad/Touchscreen

Chromebooks aren't the same as traditional computers. They have less functionalities than Windows and MacBook systems. On fact, the majority of changes are made in the laptop's Chrome browser. This may sound a little obnoxious, but it adds to the overall simplicity of the situation. Open the Chrome browser on your Chromebook to disable the touchscreen and/or touchpad.

Then, in the address bar, write "chrome:/flags/#ash-debug-shortcuts."Locate Debugging keyboard shortcuts on the following screen. It'll almost certainly be highlighted.

- To make this option active, click Enable.

Restart the device and disable the touchscreen by pressing Search + Shift + T. To turn off the touchpad, hold down Search + Shift + P. Although it may not appear so, the Chromebook touchpad has more features than a standard laptop touchpad. So, before you permanently disable the touchpad, take a look at these suggestions and try them out.

- To click, tap or press the touchpad's bottom side.

Simply press/tap the touchpad with two fingers at the same time to conduct a right-click motion. Press Alt and then click/tap with one finger as an alternative.

- To scroll, place two fingers on the touchpad and slide them left/right or up/down to conduct a horizontal or vertical scroll, respectively.

Swipe left with two fingers to return to a previously visited page. To move forward, swipe right using two fingers. Swipe down or up with three fingers to see all open windows. Hover your pointer over a tab and tap/click the touchpad with three fingers to shut it. Hover over a web link and tap/click the touchpad with three fingers to open it in a new tab. To switch between multiple tabs, swipe left/right with three fingers.

Finally, click and hold an item with one finger to transfer it from point A to point B. The item should then be dragged to the desired spot. Change the settings in the Touchpad/Touchpad and mouse section of Settings to change how the touchpad functions.

Chapter 3

An Overview of the Chrome Browser

Google released the first consumer-ready version of its Chrome web browser in late 2008, following a lengthy beta period. Google's goal was to produce a browser that could compete with established browsers like Internet Explorer, Safari, and Firefox. Chrome was released in 43 languages around the world, and it swiftly grabbed a 1% share of the web browser industry. Chrome's stripped-down style, as well as its speed and extensibility, proved appealing to a wide variety of users, from novices to techies. Other operating systems, such as Mac OS X and Linux, were quickly created for it. Chrome now accounts for 43 percent of all Internet online browsing. Web browsers are nothing more than vehicles for surfing the web at their most basic level, but on a Chromebook, your browser can do a lot more. If you're a web developer, you might have to test things out on the go while communicating with clients. You might also provide a screenshot, however the webpage you're attempting to capture contains your sensitive information. In both of these cases, the Inspect Element tool comes in handy. It enables users to change the parts of a web page's source code. Visitors and web developers can use this tool for debugging, testing, and keyword research because it is a built-in function in all major browsers. This guide will show you how to use Google Chrome's Inspect Element feature. You'll learn how to modify or conceal a page element and investigate CSS classes, among other things.

Getting to Know Chrome's Elements Panel

Chrome Developer Tools' Analyze Element feature allows you to inspect and alter a page's frontend web elements. This application allows you to edit the CSS and HTML files of a web page to change its design and content. The Developer Tools in Google Chrome can be accessed in a variety of ways. The first approach is to use the menu. Select the three vertical dots in the browser's upper right corner. Then, with your cursor hovering above More Tools, select Developer Tools. In Chrome, right-click on a page element and select Inspect, or use the Ctrl+Shift+C shortcut for Windows and Command+Shift+C shortcut for Mac to access Developer Tools. Then use Ctrl+F or Command+F to search the page's source code for anything.

The Developer Tools panel is divided into three sections:

The Document Object Model (DOM) tree for the page is displayed in the Elements/DOM panel, which also allows you full access to the HTML source code. It's commonly found in the Developer Tools' upper section.

- The CSS panel allows you to change, add, or remove CSS properties from a web page's style rules. This panel can be found in the middle of the page, directly beneath Styles.

- What's new in developer tools is displayed in Console. It's also where JavaScript runs. It can be found in the Developer Tools' bottom section.

- Other tools in Chrome Developer Tools include Source, Network, Application, Security, and more. This article will show you how to use the Elements and CSS panels to update page attributes.

What Can Chrome Developer Tools Be Used for?

The Inspect Element functionality has a lot of advantages for web developers. The following are some examples of what you can do with Elements and CSS panels: CSS live-editing allows you to view changes in the CSS panel as you make them.

Layout testing allows you to experiment with different website layouts before making permanent changes to the code. Debug diagnostics can help you figure out whether your website has any broken code. Temporary editing allows you to make changes to web page elements while they are still visible in your browser.

Why Is It Necessary to Examine Web Elements?

If you're a web developer, you can use Inspect Element to edit a site's design and examine how it looks in real time before making final changes. This saves time and improves the efficiency of client communication. Meanwhile, before capturing a snapshot, content writers can utilize the Inspect Element tool to remove sensitive information from a web page. This is more time-efficient than utilizing photo editing tools. The ability to scrutinize parts also aids search engine optimization (SEO) efforts for digital marketers. It can be used to learn about the secret keywords utilized by the competition.

How Do I Use Chrome's Inspect Element Tool?

The Inspect Element capability is now available in almost all browsers. This tutorial, on the other hand, will show you how to use it on Google Chrome.

- In Chrome, go to a website. For this lesson, we'll be using Hostinger's homepage.
- To open the drop-down menu, click the three vertical dots on Chrome's top menu bar, then pick More tools -> Developer tools.
- To quickly access the Developer tools, use the above-mentioned keyboard shortcuts or right-click on the web page and select Inspect.

You can edit the page's source code after the Elements panel displays in your browser window.

To improve readability, resize the inspector box by moving its corners. Developer tools will appear on the right side of the browser window by default. Click on the three vertical dots in the upper right corner of the panel and select the preferable Dock Side setting if you want to modify its location or move it to a separate window. Click the Toggle device toolbar in the top left corner of the panel to see how the web page looks on mobile devices. Change the variables above the preview to see how the page works at different screen resolutions or with different bandwidth throttling levels. Users can also inspect CSS classes and alter, delete, or hide site elements with Inspect Element. The parts that follow will go over how to carry out such tasks in greater detail.

Add or Remove an Element

You must edit the page's CSS or HTML source code to change a page element. You can alter the text on the page as well as its design elements, such as font weight, size, and color, this way. The text can be easily modified using the DOM panel. Use the Inspect feature (the cursor icon at the upper left of the panel) to highlight the element whose source code you want to edit after accessing the Elements box. Then, right-click on the code highlighted in the DOM tree and choose Edit as HTML from the context menu. The editor window will expand, giving you the ability to change the text. To see how the changes will look, deselect the element. A faster technique is to replace the text you want to change in the DOM panel by double-clicking it. Quotation marks are commonly used to enclose text items. It's similar to changing the style of elements, except you'll need to use the CSS panel. To highlight an element, use the Inspect tool. Then, in the upper portion of the CSS panel, click the element. Style property and add the required style declarations inside the curly brackets.

Select the element. Style attribute once more if you wish to add another style declaration.

Another blank line will be added by the web inspector for you to fill in. Here, we've added a second property that italicizes the text: When you hover your mouse over CSS properties in the CSS panel, a checkbox appears next to each of them. Uncheck this box to hide any styles you don't wish to see. You can also replace a property or a value by clicking on it.

Delete or Hide an Element

A web page's elements can also be hidden using the Developer tools. The CSS panel will add a visibility property to hide an element without destroying it when you use the Hide Element function. To do so, open the Developer Tools and use the Inspect tool to click on the element you want to conceal. Then pick Hide Element from the context menu of the code highlighted in the DOM tree. In the CSS panel, a new visibility property will emerge. To reverse the change, uncheck it.

Bookmark creation and management

In Google Chrome, how do you make bookmarks?

The bookmarks bar is hidden by default in Google Chrome, and it can only be accessed through the (...) menu. Select 'Bookmarks' and 'Show bookmarks bar' from the menu: The bookmarks bar will appear below the address bar of Google Chrome once it is enabled; if you have stored any bookmarks, they will appear in this bar:

Bookmarking a page

In Google Chrome, there are two ways to make a bookmark:

1. From the address bar icon, drag to the bookmarks bar:
2. Alternatively, go to the menu bar, pick 'bookmarks,' and then 'Bookmark this page':

Organizing bookmarks into folders

We can establish a folder for filing the bookmarks into their appropriate groupings to make organization easier. Right-click the bookmarks bar or the bookmarks menu and select 'Add folder...' to create a folder: You can drag a bookmark onto a folder by clicking and dragging it on top of it: Transferring bookmarks from one computer to another The University is now looking at bookmarks being able to automatically move between University machines for you, however until that time comes, you may want to export your bookmarks for use on another computer. The quickest way to do this is to finish building your entire list of bookmarks, then go to the 'bookmark manager' page from the menu: Once you've entered the bookmark manager, you'll notice another (...) menu on the upper right side, from which you may choose 'Export bookmarks.' After that, you'll be asked where you want to save the file. It's best if you save this to your desktop so you can find it quickly if you log onto another computer: Then, on the new computer, utilize the 'Import' button from the same menu.

How to make a Favorites list Microsoft Edge?

establishing a bookmark

To save a webpage as a bookmark or favorite link in Edge, you must first visit it. You'll see a hollow star symbol at the end of the address bar once you've arrived at the website: When you click the star symbol, a menu appears, allowing you to select a folder in which to save the bookmark:

You have the option of saving the favorite in an existing folder or creating a new one. If you want your favorite to appear on the 'bookmarks bar,' save it to the 'Favorites bar' folder.

The Favorites Bar is now visible. The Favorites bar, which is located beneath the address bar, will display the likes you've saved. This means you can get to them faster than if you went to a favorites page, which is beneficial for frequently used links. You must enable it from the "..." option on the upper right of the browser in order for it to appear. You can enable the 'Show favorites bar' button by going to 'Settings' and then 'View favorite settings.'

Firefox

To store a website as a bookmark or favorite link in the Firefox browser, you must first visit it. You'll see a hollow star symbol at the end of the address bar once you've arrived at the website: When you click the star sign, you'll see a menu that allows you to: You may also give the bookmark a name and put it in a folder of your choice. You can also add tags to the bookmark so that you can find it later. The Bookmarks bar appears. Click the 'book icons' at the end of the address bar to bring up the bookmarks bar below the address bar: Select 'bookmarks', then 'bookmarking tools,' and finally' show bookmarks bar' from this menu: The information that Internet Explorer saves on a computer as you visit the web is known as your browsing history. This includes information you've entered into forms, passwords, and websites you've visited to help optimize your experience. If you're using a shared or public computer, though, you might not want Internet Explorer to preserve your browsing history.

View your surfing history and remove certain websites from your list. You can erase certain websites or return to a webpage you've already visited by examining your browsing history.

Select the Favorites button in Internet Explorer.

Select the Past tab, and then select a filter from the drop-down box to determine how you want to view your history. To remove a specific site from one of these lists, right-click it and select Delete. Alternatively, select any site from the list to return to a previous page.

Delete your internet history.

Delete your browsing history on a regular basis to preserve your privacy, especially if you use a shared or public computer. Select the Tools button in Internet Explorer, navigate to Safety, and then select Delete browsing history.

Select the data or files you want to delete from your computer, and then click Delete.

Chapter 4

Getting Your Hands on the Keyboard and Touchpad

It's difficult to say whether Christopher Latham Sholes anticipated his keyboard's design and letter layout remaining in use well into the twenty-first century. Regardless of what his original intentions were, his legacy continues to live on today. Sholes intended to decrease typewriter jams and speed up the typist when he designed the layout and functioning of the keyboard we use today. (However, some claimed that the altered letter layout was intended to slow down the typist and therefore reduce typewriter jams.)

The keyboard hasn't changed much in the last 140 years. The basic arrangement of letters and numbers has remained same; the only significant changes have been the addition of multi-purpose keys such as the? / key and the:; key. Keys like Caps Lock and Shift, as well as function keys, became popular with the introduction of word processors and computers.

Taking a Look at the Keyboard and Touchpad

A numeric keypad is used to control your mouse.

To access your computer's accessibility options, click Windows logo key or go to Start > Settings > Accessibility.

Select the mouse pointer and press the touch button. Adjust the Size slider under Mouse pointer until your mouse pointer is the size you want. Change the color of your mouse pointer to white, black, inverted, or any of the brilliant recommended colors under Mouse pointer style.

Choose another color to change the color of the pointer.

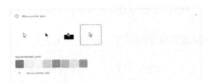

Make your text cursor more visible.

Change the thickness of the text cursor and add a colored indicator to make it more visible in Windows 11. Thickness of the text cursor can be changed. To access your computer's accessibility options, click Windows logo key+U or go to Start > Settings > Accessibility.

Choose the Text cursor.

Adjust the Text cursor thickness slider under Text cursor thickness until the thickness in the preview seems right. Use the text cursor indication to help you find what you're looking for. To access your computer's accessibility options, click Windows logo key+U or go to Start > Settings > Accessibility. Switch on the Text cursor indication. Adjust the Size slider until the preview shows the size you want. To alter the color of the indicator, select one from the Recommended colors menu, or choose a custom color from the Choose another color option.

Cursor settings for text

Make the keyboard more user-friendly.

To access your computer's accessibility options, click Windows logo key+U or go to Start > Settings > Accessibility. Choose Keyboard and experiment with some of the following options: Turn on the On-screen keyboard switch to pick keys with the mouse or another pointing device (such as a joystick) or to cycle between the keys on the screen with a single switch. If you have problems pressing two keys at the same time, turn on the Sticky keys switch. Sticky keys allow you to press one key at a time actions that need several keys (such as Ctrl + S). When you press the Caps lock, Num lock, or Scroll lock keys, the Toggle keys switch will play a sound. Set the keyboard's sensitivity to overlook brief or repetitive keystrokes by turning on the Filter keys switch. When available, turn on the Underline access keys switch to underline access keys. To use the Prt Scr button to open screen snipping, toggle the Use the Print Screen button to open screen snipping switch on.

Getting to know shortcut keys

A keyboard shortcut is a set of keys that you can press to do a specific task on your computer. In written writing, keys that are meant to be pressed at the same moment are usually connected by a

+. Ctrl+S, for example, indicates that you should simultaneously hit the Ctrl and S keys. There is a plethora of keyboard shortcuts available. However, you will most likely just need a few. Many of these shortcuts will be used throughout the course.

SHORTCUTS THAT ARE MOST COMMONLY APPLIED

CommandShortcutExplanationCutCtrl+XCopies and removes an item or text; used with PasteCopyCtrl+CCopies an item or text; used with PastePasteCtrl+VInserts the last cut or copied item or textSelect AllCtrl+ASelects all text or itemsUndoCtrl+ZUndoes the last actionRedoCtrl+YRedoes the last thing undoneTroubleshoot/Force QuitCtrl+Alt+DeleteOpens Task Manager (see note)Close windowAlt+F4Closes window; shuts down computer if all windows are closedNewCtrl+NOpens a new window, tab, or documentOpenCtrl+OOpens a file or documentSaveCtrl+SSaves a fileFind Ctrl+FOpens search tools; in most programs, opens a search box to find specific words on a page

Changing the settings on your keyboard and touchpad

Despite the fact that your touchpad is a permanent element of your laptop, your computer perceives it as an external device to some extent. You must first access your touchpad's driver, which governs the touchpad's interactions with your operating system, in order to adjust its settings. The settings options on the pad differ depending on the model. Some pads allow you to tap program shortcuts in the corners, while others interpret finger motions as commands. Most pads have edges that may be used to scroll over documents, making it easier to navigate extensive Web pages and business reports.

1. Select "Control Panel" from the Windows "Start" menu.

2. Select "Hardware and Sound" from the drop-down menu to see a collection of hardware setting tools.

3. In the Devices and Printers section of the window, click "Mouse" to open the Mouse Properties dialog box.

4. Select "Device Settings" from the drop-down menu.

5. To access the Settings dialog box for your driver, click "Settings."

6. Adjust the settings on your touchpad, which vary based on the brand and model.

Sensitivity and speed options are frequently included.

It's simple to connect your keyboard and mouse to your computer. Before connecting your keyboard and mouse to your computer, you must first decide where the keyboard and mouse will be placed in relation to the computer: Place the keyboard between you and the monitor, directly in front of where you'll sit when using the computer. Depending on whether you're right- or left-handed, the mouse is either to the right or left of the keyboard. You can now connect your mouse and keyboard once you've placed them where you want them: The PC keyboard connects to the console's keyboard connector on the back. The mouse is connected to the mouse port.

Chapter 5

Exploring Chromebook Apps

Google's original intention for the Chromebook was to develop a computer that did the majority of its work over the Internet, the Chromebook runs almost entirely on the Chrome web browser. Applications aren't installed on Chromebooks way they are on Windows or Mac computers; instead, they are kept on remote computers and accessed via the Internet. Google offers a variety of web-based applications to assist you with work, school, personal growth, entertainment, and other activities. Because the Chromebook doesn't require expensive hardware to execute the programs, this notion — employing online applications and eliminating the need to install software locally — saves money for both Google and the consumer.

This chapter gives you a quick rundown of the apps that come preinstalled on your Chromebook, as well as instructions on how to search and add new apps to your App Launcher. Remember that installing apps on your Chromebook is as simple as adding a shortcut to your menu and tweaking a few settings.

Educational Learning Apps' Advantages

The education sector has seen a significant expansion of technology in the aftermath of the global epidemic. The entire industry is discovering new methods of doing things thanks to technology. It's not that technology hasn't been used in education before; it just hasn't been employed in educational applications. Using technology was once an option, but it is now a necessity. As a result, instructional software creation via mobile applications has become popular, allowing businesses, particularly in the education sector, to achieve new heights. It was clear that there was a high demand for technical tools and systems that allowed professors to engage with their students, track their learning progress, and distribute their courses during compulsory distance learning.

What Does It Mean to Learn On the Go?

Students could previously only receive an education in a physical classroom, but mobile learning allowed students to attend classes via cellphones, tablets, and laptops. By downloading assignments and uploading completed homework, students can access the learning process at any time and from any location. Mobile learning is sweeping the globe, and education is expanding at a breakneck speed. There are many benefits to mobile learning, but there are also some drawbacks.

What Are the Benefits of Using Mobile Apps to Learn?

There are numerous benefits to learning using the top learning apps for kids, including:

1. Educational Technologies of the Future

As a result of the introduction of applications in the education sector, new learning curricula have arisen. Fun activities that involve youngsters in a healthy mental process and help them see things from a different perspective can be found in mobile applications.

2. Unspecified Purposes

Mobile applications can be utilized for a range of different student-related functions, such as making online school fee payments and other payments. It eliminates the need to pay school fees and stand in line. Furthermore, attendance management applications maintain track of students' attendance so that teachers can monitor it. It makes it simple for teachers and parents to keep track of student attendance.

3. Learning is possible at any time and in any location.

Students who engage in learning activities have access to materials long after they have left the school grounds. Educators can connect with their students online, administer assessments, and give additional materials, such as instructive movies, for them to watch in their leisure time. When students are asked to perform independently and on their own terms, they become more engaged in the learning process. Making information available for kids to access later is also a good way to avoid spending time on the internet. Using additional resources outside of the classroom helps students stay focused on their learning goals and, in many circumstances, improves their performance when they return to the classroom.

4. The Easiest Method of Instruction

The tutorial promotes a straightforward instructional approach that yields the finest results. Teachers no longer need to be concerned about their students' attention spans because educational applications provide a visually appealing User Interface that allows students to interact with their devices. Additionally, students can download the full unit to their mobile phones, guaranteeing that the syllabus is completed on time.

5. Keep an eye on your kids' progress.

Many apps allow you to keep track of your children's progress, which is something that every parent wants to know. You can observe how each program improves your children's reading, math, and other skills over time.

6. There Are No Apps, Only Children

It's a prevalent misperception that apps are solely useful for teenagers. Both teachers and parents gain from the use of educational software. The apps can be used in the classroom by teachers. Teachers can use apps to assist them construct lesson plans. With app-based learning, teachers and parents have more time to discuss lesson plans, resulting in more interactive sessions. When it comes to selecting apps for children, parents and teachers may make a significant difference.

7. Study Resources on the Internet

Thanks to online lessons and eBooks, students' lives are made easier and less stressful. Thanks to technological advancements, students can now access a large choice of books with a simple click. If your child has an educational app on their phone, they will be able to access all of the books that are available on it, and it will fit easily in their pockets. Learners, on the other hand, do not need to purchase books or study materials because they may obtain them everything online.

8. Use eBooks and the Internet to Study

Students are becoming more interested in online learning these days. Apps for searching the library and finding books come in handy in this situation. These features make it simple for students to locate the appropriate course resources on the mobile app. It helps individuals organize their study resources online and puts them closer to the study materials.

9. There Is a Communication Gap Between Students and The Institution

Traditional practices, it could be argued, do not allow institutes to provide equal attention to all students. It is, however, now possible to do so. Information can be sent to all pupils via school communication apps. They can keep students informed about new schedules, forums, conferences, and social events at school.

Mobile Apps Have Additional Educational Benefits

- The following are some of the advantages:
- They provide an opportunity for debate.
- Students' interest in learning is sparked by the usage of mobile devices, especially those who lacked enthusiasm during a traditional presentation.

- They enable information exchange and learning without the need for an internet connection.
- They can sort data to make searching easier depending on particular parameters.
- They enable practical work with a variety of technologies—students have access to resources that include not just information about the topic being studied, but also extra knowledge and the ability to use a variety of technologies, allowing them to achieve the necessary degree of education.
- They provide an overview of the many types of resources (visual and audio educational materials).
- They provide the opportunity for development in accordance with the times.

Taking a look at some of the pre-installed apps

A lot of apps are pre-installed on every Android device. These are apps that Google or the maker of your smartphone wants you to use. Some of them may be necessary, but what about the pre-installed apps you never use? Bloatware is a term used to describe undesirable Android apps that can't be deleted using the standard uninstall process. We'll show you how to uninstall pre-installed apps on Android without rooting your device in this article. But first, try turning off the default apps.

Disable Apps That Have Already Been Installed

Pre-installed apps can be disabled by some smartphone makers. The app will not be deleted from your phone, but it will cease running in the background and no longer appear in the app drawer. Go to Settings > Apps & notifications > See all apps to disable an app on your Android device. Now select the program you wish to turn off and press the Disable button. Depending on the Android smartphone you're using, this technique may differ. You won't be able to uninstall the app if you don't see the Disable button or an option that says "Uninstall updates." You can get rid of it by following the steps outlined below.

How to Get Rid of Android Bloatware

ADB must be installed on your Android device in order to delete pre-loaded apps. For more information, see our guide on how to utilize ADB and Fastboot on Android. For convenience of use, you can download the minimum ADB setup from xda-developers.com if you're running Windows. You must to activate USB debugging on your Android smartphone before proceeding. Go to Settings > About Phone on your Android device. Then tap the Build number numerous times to access the Developer settings. Now, go to Developer settings and enable USB debugging (which is normally found under System or Additional Settings). Once ADB is installed and USB debugging is allowed, you can remove bloatware from Android by following the instructions below:

- Use a USB cord to connect your Android handset to your computer.
- Open the command prompt on your computer.
- In the command prompt, type adb devices and hit Enter.
- On your smartphone, you'll see a prompt asking you to allow a connection with the computer. Select OK.
- Enter the command adb devices once more. Your device will now appear in the "List of devices attached" section.

Press Enter after typing adb shell. To uninstall an undesired app, type pm uninstall -k —user 0 package name>. The name of the file that contains the software you're uninstalling is referred to as the package name in this situation. What makes you think you know what that is? Download App Inspector from the Play Store for free on your Android smartphone. The package name of the program you want to delete can then be found using this method. You may also use the command adb shell cmd package install-existing name of package> to reinstall a default app.

Things to Keep in Mind

This approach lets you to delete all of your Android device's default apps, including the system apps. If you're planning to delete system apps, make sure that their absence won't affect the device's or other apps' functionality. This approach can also only be used to uninstall pre-installed programs for the current user. In other words, if you reboot your device, the uninstalled apps will resurface. To uninstall undesired apps for all users, you'll need root access. You can use Google Play apps on any Android smartphone without having to pay again. Each device, however, must use the same Google Account. You can do the following: Installing an app on several Android devices is possible. On a new Android device, install an app. Reinstall a program that you previously purchased but then deleted. You can also reactivate an app that arrived with your device if it was turned off.

Apps can be reinstalled or turned back on.

Open Google Play Store on your Android phone or tablet. Tap the profile icon on the right. Go to Manage Apps & Devices and select Manage Apps & Devices. Manage. Choose whatever apps you want to install or activate. If you can't find the app, tap Installed Not installed at the top. Select Install or Enable from the drop-down menu.

Chapter 6

Finding Your Files

Chrome OS is a small, light operating system that doesn't take up a lot of space and doesn't require a lot of resources to run. This is, of course, intentional. Google set intended to build a low-cost, high-utility computer that worked in tandem with the Google platform. Because your Chromebook just runs web programs, there's no need for a lot of storage. As a result, Chromebooks' hard drives are often less than 32GB. Although you won't be able to install many apps on the Chromebook itself, you will require some storage.

For example, you could wish to use your Chromebook camera to download a file attachment from an email, or to take a screen shot or capture some video footage or stills. You'll need more than just storage space for these data; you'll also require access to them. Windows

Explorer is what you'd use to search for files on your Windows PC. If you're using a Mac, you'll utilize the Finder.

Using the Files application

If you use a Chromebook for any kind of productivity-related work, you'll want to be aware of these advanced file wizardry techniques. So take your virtual wand and get ready for the following: It's time to give your Chrome OS experience a whole new level of efficiency. Although Chrome OS is centered on Google software and services, you don't have to limit yourself to Google Drive for online storage. So here's the key to remembering it:

Install and set up the official Android app for whatever provider you wish to add to the mix if you want your Chromebook to integrate with other cloud storage alternatives. Once you've set up the Chrome OS Files app and signed in, as long as the service supports the Chrome OS file system standard — which popular office choices like Dropbox and OneDrive do — it'll display as an accessible option within the app.

- Dropbox, OneDrive, and other cloud services may be integrated directly into the Chrome OS file system with a few simple clicks. (To enlarge any image in this story, click on it.)
- Speaking of cloud storage, Chromebooks have an odd mismatch in that the systems are theoretically all about the cloud and keeping your data constantly synced — but any things you download from the web are actually saved in a local device folder by default. You can correct this by typing chrome: settings into any open browser window's address bar, then selecting "Advanced" followed by "Downloads" from

the left sidebar menu. In the main part of the screen, look for the line labeled "Location" and click the Change button next to it. Then, under your Google Drive storage, simply select a folder (or create a new folder exclusively for downloads).

That way, anything you download in Chrome will be saved to Drive and accessible from everywhere you sign in. (And, yes, using the preceding suggestion, you can do the same thing with any other cloud storage service.)

- If you really want to go all out, you can boost your Chromebook's cloud-connecting power even more by syncing downloads with the same Drive folder on your Windows or Mac computer and Android phone, thus establishing a single device-agnostic and internet-based "Downloads" folder. That way, whatever you download from anyplace will always be available on your current device. If you dare, you may find the complete instructions in this Android Intelligence column.

- In the Chrome OS Quick Settings panel, look for the "Nearly visibility" option if you need to transfer a file to or from another Chromebook or between your current Chromebook and an Android device (in the lower-right corner of the screen). This will enable you to configure and activate Google's Nearby Share feature, which is accessible on both Chrome OS and Android and allows you to wirelessly transfer files across devices.

- In the left panel of your Chromebook's Files app, you can build custom shortcuts to frequently used folders — from either your local storage or any connected cloud service — for easy access. Within that panel, find the folder you want and right-click it, then pick "Pin folder" to add it to the list.

- Use the Chrome OS Tote section, which is located to the left of the clock in the bottom-of-screen status bar region, to make a file even readily accessible. (It's the icon that resembles a box with a downward-pointing arrow inside.) You may pin certain files or folders to the Tote section by pulling them up in the main panel of the Files app, right-clicking their names, and then selecting "Pin to shelf" from the menu that displays.

Pinning files or folders to your Chromebook's Tote area ensures that they're always just a click or tap away.

- While we're on the subject of the Files app, here's a handy shortcut: By pressing Shift-Alt-M, you can access the Chromebook's file manager at any time and from any location.
- Make a mental note: The next time you're in the Files app, press Ctrl and then the number keys that correspond to their position to switch between different sections

(Ctrl-1 for Recent, Ctrl-3 for Images, and so on).

- Here's a quick way to rename files and folders on your Chromebook that can save you time: To modify the name of an object highlighted in the Chrome OS Files app, use Ctrl and Enter. There's no need to waste time clicking, searching through menus, or wasting seconds.

- The Files app in Chrome OS includes some built-in photo enhancing features that are ideal for simple image alteration and markups. To begin, simply seek for the Crop & Rotate, Rescale, Lighting Filters, and Annotate buttons towards the top of the screen while viewing an image in Files.

The built-in Files app on your Chromebook provides some useful features for quickly editing and tagging up photographs.

- Give your Chromebook the Solid Explorer Android app for an even more powerful file management experience (also my pick for the best advanced file manager app on Android). It's built for Chrome OS, and it features a two-panel view for dragging and dropping files between several locations, including your ordinary Chrome OS storage, a portion of your storage allocated for Android apps, and a wide range of cloud-based storage accounts. You may also use it to add additional encryption to specific files or folders, as well as construct password-protected ZIP or 7ZIP archives. After a two-week trial, the app costs $3.

Are you ready for some sophisticated Chromebook magic? Discover all sorts of handy shortcuts for getting around Chrome OS, managing apps and windows, increasing your text input, and more in this list of 50 tips for optimal Chromebook productivity.

Using your Chromebook's external storage

On portable devices, Chrome OS supports a variety of file systems. It supports the FAT16, FAT32, and exFAT file systems, which are cross-platform. It also has complete read and write functionality for the Windows NTFS file system. It can also read but not write to the Mac HFS+ file system. Chromebooks support the MTP protocol for digital cameras and music players, and Chromebooks can read ISO9660 and UDF file systems on external disc drives connected through USB. You should probably format your external drive as exFAT. In fact, if you format a USB drive or SD card from within Chrome OS, the device will be formatted as exFAT without even prompting you to choose a file system.

How to Work with Files and Access a Drive

Connect an external storage device to your Chromebook and launch the Files app to use it on Chrome OS. The drive will display in the left pane of the files app, below Google Drive and the Downloads folder, which houses all of your Chromebook's local files. You may either drag and drop files from the Downloads folder or Google Drive into the drive, or right-click them, select "Copy," and then right-click on the drive, select "Paste." When downloading a file on Chrome OS, you can opt to save it directly to an external drive using the "Save As" window.

Ctrl+A selects all files, Ctrl+C copies files, Ctrl+X cuts files, and Ctrl+V pastes files, among other keyboard shortcuts. To create a new folder on the drive, right-click inside it and select "New Folder"– or press Ctrl+E. You can change the display to a grid of thumbnail previews instead of a list of files and sort the files by file name, size, type, or date changed using the settings in the top right corner of the window. There's also a search function for discovering files quickly. Many files can be opened straight from the external drive, including films, music files, photos, PDFs, and other documents. Simply save them to your hard disk and double-click them.

How to Determine the Amount of Storage Space Available

Select your external drive in the left pane and then click the menu button in the top right corner of the Files window to see how much storage space it has. You'll be able to check how much room is remaining. To free up space on your hard drive, delete files. This method can also be used to determine how much storage space is available on your Chromebook. Simply click the menu button after selecting the "Downloads" folder.

What Is the Best Way to Format a Hard Drive?

Right-click the drive's name and select "Format Device" to erase and format it. Chrome OS will use the exFAT file system to format the drive. There's no option to select a new file system, change the partition arrangement, or give the drive a different name.

Ejecting a Hard Drive

When you're done operating the drive, make sure to remove it from your Chromebook before removing it. This prevents data loss by verifying that your Chromebook has finished writing to the hard disk before removing it. It's also why you should "safely remove" disks in Windows. To do so, either right-click the drive and select "Eject Device" or click the "Eject" button to the right of the drive's name in the Files App. External storage devices operate fine with Chrome OS, however there aren't many more capabilities. For example, you can't partition or rename your device without using a Windows, Mac, or Linux computer. A DVD drive can be connected to your Chromebook via

USB connection, but you can only access the files on it. It's impossible to watch copy-protected DVD movies without first ripping them. An external drive, on the other hand, will suffice if all you need is some extra space.

Getting started with Google Drive and using it

1. Go to drive.google.com on your PC. You'll see "My Drive," which contains the following items: Data and folders you upload or sync Google Docs, Sheets, Slides, and Forms you create Learn how to back up and sync files from your Mac or PC.
2. Create or upload files

You can use Google Drive to upload files from your computer or to create new ones. Google Drive allows you to upload files and directories.

Working with Office documents

Create, format, and edit Google Docs, Sheets, and Slides are all free to use.

3. Organize and share files

Other people can view, modify, and comment on files or folders that you share.

- Google Drive files can be shared.
- Google Drive folders can be shared.
- Change the owner of a file to someone else.

Chapter 7

Proceeding with Word Processing

Chromebooks aren't simply for entertainment. It's a useful tool for both students and professionals. However, it is the Chromebook's free access to — and perfect integration with — the Google platform that makes it so powerful. The Google platform's web-based office tools are a major component. Google Docs is a term that is frequently used to refer to the full suite of these products, albeit informally. However, Docs is also the official name of Google's web-based word processing product inside that suite, which can be misleading. When I say Google Docs in this book, I'm referring to Google's word processor.

Docs is a robust word processor with a wide range of features. This chapter's objective isn't to delve into each detail of the Docs application. Instead,

I'll focus on the fundamentals. You should be able to open and create documents, write, format, and otherwise alter text, and save, export, and share them by the end of this chapter. While the ability to collaborate on a project from different locations is undoubtedly the most appealing feature of Google Docs, the true beauty of a Google Doc is how it protects your work from being lost in the event of a computer crash or human error. Google Docs saves itself practically constantly and backs up to a remote place, so you'll never lose a file unless you delete it on purpose.

Consider switching from Word or Pages to a Google Doc if you're working on a report, term paper, or work assignment that you can't afford to lose. You can always copy and paste your work from Google into another software later, but you'll never be able to recover a document that was unintentionally erased. However, for most people, the ability to collaborate on a document with a large group of people is the most appealing feature. You can either create a Google Doc and then share it with others for editing or adding material later, or you can share the document right away and collaborate in real time, watching as your colleague's type, edit, revise, and work on it.

On your computer, how to make a Google Doc

1. Log in to your Google account by going to Google.com, Gmail, or Google Drive.
2. At the upper right of the screen, click the Google Apps icon, which is a square comprised by nine smaller dark gray squares.

To get started, go to this page and click the applications button.

3. Scroll down to the second group of program icons and pick the "Docs" icon, which is blue with white stripes.

Select "Docs" from the drop-down menu.

4. On the following screen, select the sort of document you wish to create, keeping in mind that the first option, the "Blank" page with the multicolored plus symbol, is the most common.

For your document, select a template format.

5. Your new Google document appears when you click on the "Blank" doc.

A blank page is waiting for you.

After you've created a Google Doc, the first thing you should do is give it a name by putting a new title into the top-left bar, which will auto-fill with "Untitled Document." After then, if others are expecting you to do so, share it. You must first download the Google Docs app to your mobile device in order to create a Google Doc. The quickest approach to locate the app is to download it from Apple's Software Store or your device's similar app marketplace.

Sign into Google from your mobile web browser and then tap the Google Apps button in the top right corner of your screen to access the app. If you swipe down and tap the "Docs" symbol, you'll be sent to a screen with a prominent "Download Google Docs" link. Then click it to download the app.

Once you've downloaded the Google Docs app to your phone, follow these steps:

1. Open the app to see all of the previous documents that have been provided to you.

2. Click the colorful + symbol in the bottom right corner of the screen to create a new Google Doc.

To make a new document, click the multicolored + symbol.

3. Select "New document" or "Choose template" from the drop-down menu.

Create a new document or use a template.

4. Begin typing.

If you know where they're stored, use the folder icon at the top right of the app's home screen to find them, or use the magnifying glass symbol beside it to search by name.

Text formatting and manipulation

Using Microsoft Word to format and edit text in a document You'll probably want to revise and format your document once you've typed it into Microsoft Word to make it more presentable. Word's best feature is that it underlines any mistakes you've made, whether they're typos, misspellings, or grammar mistakes. As you enter, some typos will be automatically rectified. For example, if you input the word 'exampel,' Word will automatically correct it. You might not even notice you've made a mistake thanks to the program's auto-correct option.

In MS Word, you may check your spelling and grammar. It is recommended that you utilize the spelling and grammar check capabilities after you have finished typing a document. This can be accomplished in two ways. You can check the supplied suggestions by right-clicking on the underlined word or phrase, then selecting the correct one. You can use the grammar and spelling checker. Select Spelling and Grammar from the Tools menu. When you need to spell check a large amount of text, this tool comes in helpful. You can find the proper corrections by looking through the list of suggested terms. Words that aren't in the dictionary can be ignored. You may also expand the dictionary by adding new terms.

How to Format a Word Document

You can modify the font, font style, font color, and font size in your document by formatting it. To format text, you must first choose it. The following methods can be used to select or highlight text. Click at the start of your text, then drag to the finish while holding down the left mouse button. Place your cursor at the start of your text. Move the right arrow key while holding down the shift key until you reach the end of your text. To move to the next sentence, press the down arrow.

- Click at the start of your text, then hold down the shift key while clicking at the end.
- Double-click on a word to select it.
- Triple-click a paragraph to select it as a whole.
- To select a whole document, click three times on its margin.
- Select All from the Edit menu, or hold down the CTRL key and press A.
- Select Font from the Format menu after successfully highlighting the text you wish to format.

You may alter a lot of things about the font in the dialogue box that appears. Documents can be saved, exported, and shared. Save as and Save as new. Save and Save As are the two options for saving a file in Word. These choices operate in a similar manner, with a few key distinctions.

Save: You'll use the Save command to save your changes when you're creating or editing a document. The majority of the time, you'll use this command. You'll only have to specify a file name and location the first time you save a file. After that, you may save it with the same name and location by using the Save command.

Save As: This command is used to make a duplicate of a document while maintaining the original. When you choose Save As, you'll need to give the cloned version a new name and/or location.

OneDrive for Business

The majority of Microsoft Office capabilities, including Word, are designed to save and share documents online. OneDrive, an online storage space for your documents and files, is used for this. Make sure you're signed in to Word with your

Microsoft account if you wish to use OneDrive. To learn more, take a look at our lecture on OneDrive.

To save a document, follow these steps:

When you start a new project or make modifications to an existing one, it's critical to save your work. Early and frequent saving can help you avoid losing your work. You should also pay attention to where you store the document so that it is easier to locate afterwards. On the Quick Access Toolbar, find and pick the Save command.

The Save As pane will appear in Backstage view if you're saving the file for the first time. After that, you'll need to decide where to save the file and give it a name. To select a location on your computer, click Browse. You can also save the file to your OneDrive account by clicking OneDrive.

You'll see the Save As dialog box pop up. Choose the location where you wish the document to be saved. After that, save the document by giving it a name.

The file is about to be saved. As you make changes to the document, you can click the Save option again to save your modifications. You can also use your keyboard to access the Save function by hitting Ctrl+S.

To make a copy, use Save As.

You can make a copy of a document to save a new version while maintaining the original. For example, if you have a file called Sales Report, you may rename it Sales Report 2 so that you can update the new file while still referring to the original. To do so, go to Backstage view and click the Save As instruction. You'll need to choose where to store the file and give it a new file name, just as when storing a file for the first time. To change the default save location: If you don't want to utilize OneDrive, you could be annoyed that it is chosen as the default save destination. If this is difficult for you, you can change the default save location to This PC by default.

Backstage view can be accessed by clicking the File tab.

Select Options from the dropdown menu.

A dialog box called Word Options will emerge. On the left, click Save, then check the box next to Save to Computer by Default. Finally, click OK.

The default location for saving data will be modified.

Auto Recover

While you're working on a document, Word automatically saves it to a temporary folder. If you forget to save your changes or Word crashes, you can use AutoRecover to recover the file.

To utilize AutoRecover, follow these steps:

Open a new Word document. The Document Recovery window will show on the left if autosaved versions of a file are found. To open a file, simply click it. The document will be returned to you.

Word saves automatically every 10 minutes by default. Word may not create an autosaved version if you are altering a document for less

than 10 minutes. If you can't find the file you're looking for, go to Backstage view and look through all autosaved files. Select the File tab, then Manage Versions, then Recover Unsaved Documents from the drop-down menu.

Documents to be exported

Word documents are stored in the.docx format by default. However, you may need to utilize a different file type, such as a PDF or a Word 97-2003 document, at times. It's simple to export your Word document to a variety of file formats.

To save a document as a PDF, follow these steps: If you're sharing a document with someone who doesn't have Word, exporting it as an Adobe Acrobat document, often known as a PDF file, can be extremely handy. Recipients will be able to see, but not alter, the content of your document if it is saved as a PDF file.

- To access Backstage view, click the File tab, then Export, then Create PDF/XPS. You'll see the Save As dialog box pop up. Choose where you want to save the document, give it a name, and then click Publish.

Word allows you to convert a PDF file into an editable document if you need to make changes to it. For more information, see our guide on Editing PDF Files. To convert a document to a different file format, follow these steps: You might also find it useful to export your document to other file types, such as a Word 97-2003 Document if you need to share it with individuals who use an older version of Word or a.txt file if you only need a plain-text version. To reach Backstage view, click the File tab, then Export, then Change File Type. After choosing a file type, click Save As. You'll see the Save As dialog box pop up. Choose where you want to save the document, give it a name, and then click Save.

You may also save documents to a variety of file types by using the Save As type drop-down menu in the Save As dialog box.

Document sharing

Using OneDrive, Word makes it simple to share and collaborate on documents. You could send a file as an email attachment in the past if you wanted to share it with someone. While this technique is convenient, it also creates many copies of the same file, making it difficult to keep track of. When you share a Word document, you're essentially granting people access to the same document. This allows you and the individuals with whom you share the document to work on it together without having to keep track of numerous versions. To share a document, you must first save it to your OneDrive account.

To share a document, go to Backstage view, then click Share on the File tab.

A window called Send Link will appear.

To discover more about the many ways to share a document, use the buttons in the interactive below.

To make a copy of the document, go to File > Save As. Save Challenge Practice is the name of the new copy. You can store it to your computer's folder or to your OneDrive account. Make a PDF of your document.

Chapter 8

Summarizing Sheets

Accounting and other corporate finance–related mathematical operations were done with good old paper and pencil before the computer era. Accounting spreadsheets had rows and columns that intersected to form cells, allowing for on-sheet organization. Calculations may then be conducted and written into appropriate cells in separate rows and columns, with each cell containing some sort of value. Personal computers revolutionized the way firms and finance professionals did business when they first appeared on the scene. Digital spreadsheets make it easy to enter data and generate results automatically.

New spreadsheet creation

A workbook is a document that contains one or more worksheets to aid with data organization. A blank workbook or a template can be used to start a new workbook. A workbook is a document that contains one or more worksheets to aid with data organization. A blank workbook or a template can be used to start a new workbook.

- Make yourself a workbook.
- Excel should now be open.
- Press Ctrl+N or select Blank workbook.
- Begin typing.
- Make a workbook using a template.
- Choose File > New from the File menu.
- Double-click a template to open it.
- Start typing after clicking.

Numbers, Dates, and Times Formatting

Displaying your data in a logical, consistent, and easy format is one of the best methods to increase the readability of your worksheets. You can improve your spreadsheet style by formatting currency amounts with leading dollar signs, percentages with trailing percent signs, and huge figures with commas, to name a few examples. This section explains how to use Excel's built-in formatting tools to format numbers, dates, and timings. You'll also learn how to develop your own formats so you may have complete control over how your data appears.

Formats for displaying numbers

Excel removes any leading or trailing zeros when you enter numbers in a worksheet. If you type 0123.4500 into Excel, it will appear 123.45. When you enter a number that is larger than the cell, this rule is broken. In this scenario, Excel normally widens the column to accommodate the number. Excel, on the other hand, tailors the number to suit the cell in some circumstances by rounding off some decimal points. A number like 123.45678, for example, is represented as 123.4568. Note that the number is simply modified for display purposes in this example; Excel keeps the original number internally. By default, each cell in a worksheet uses this format, known as the General number format. If you want your numbers to look different, you can choose from one of Excel's seven numerical formats: Number, currency, accounting, percentage, fraction, scientific, and special are all terms that can be used to describe something.

Formats for numbers— The number of decimal places, whether the thousands separator (,) is used, and how negative numbers are shown are the three components of the number formats. If the number is negative, it can be displayed with a leading minus sign, in red, surrounded by parenthesis, or in red, surrounded by parentheses. Currency formats are similar to number formats, with the exception that the thousands separator is always used, and you can show the numbers with a leading dollar sign ($) or another currency symbol.

Accounting forms—You can choose the number of decimal places and whether or not to display a leading dollar sign using accounting formats (or other currency symbol). If you use a dollar sign in a cell, Excel shows it flush left. Parentheses are used to surround all negative entries. Percentage formats show a number multiplied by 100 with a percent sign (percent) to the right of the number. For instance,.506 is shown as 50.6 percent. Up to 14 decimal places can be displayed.

Fraction formats—You can express decimal amounts as fractions using fraction formats. There are nine different fraction formats available, including halves, quarters, eighths, sixteenths, tenths, and hundredths.

Scientific formats—The most significant number appears to the left of the decimal, followed by 2–30 decimal places to the right of the decimal, and finally the exponent. As a result, 123000 is shown as 1.23E+05.

Formats that are unique—The special formats are a group of files created to deal with unique situations. Here's a rundown of the many formats, along with some examples:

Changing the Format of Numeric Values

Specifying the format as you enter your data is the quickest approach to format numbers. If you start a dollar figure with a dollar sign ($), Excel formats the value as currency automatically. Similarly, Excel automatically transforms a number as a percentage when you type a percent sign (%) after it. Here are some additional instances of how this strategy can be used. You can use either the negative symbol (−) or parentheses to enter a negative value.

Number Entered	Number Displayed	Format Used
$1234.567	$1,234.57	Currency
($1234.5)	($1,234.50)	Currency
10%	10%	Percentage
123E+02	1.23E+04	Scientific
5 3/4	5 3/4	Fraction
0 3/4	3/4	Fraction
3/4	4-Mar	Date

Because Excel guesses the format you want to use, specifying the numeric format as you enter a number is quick and efficient. Excel, unfortunately, makes mistakes from time to time (for example, interpreting a simple fraction as a date). In any case, you don't have access to all of the formats that are offered (for example, displaying negative dollar amounts in red). To get around these limits, you can choose from a list of number forms. The steps are as follows:

- Choose the cell or range of cells to which the new format should be applied.
- The Home tab should be selected.
- Select Number Format from the drop-down menu.
- Excel shows you how the current cell would be displayed if you choose that format under the name of each format.

Pull down the Number Format list on the Home tab to see all of Excel's built-in numeric formats.

Choose the format you'd like to use.

Use the Number tab of the Format Cells dialog box for further numeric formatting options. Choose Home, Number Format, More Number Formats after selecting the cell or range. (Alternatively, press Ctrl+1 or click the Number group's dialog box launcher.) When you pick a number format in the Category list, Excel offers further formatting options, such as the Decimal Places spin box, as (The choices you see are determined by the category you choose.) The Sample information box displays an example of how the format was applied to the contents of the current cell.

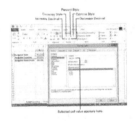

Excel displays the format's options when you select a format from the Category list. Excel provides numerous keyboard shortcuts for adjusting the numeric format as an alternative to using the Format Cells dialog box. Use one of the key combinations indicated in Table 3.6 to format the cell or range you want to format.

Shortcut Keys for Selecting Numeric Formats

Shortcut Key	Format
Ctrl+~	General
Ctrl+~	Number (two decimal places; using thousands separator)

Numeric Formats Can Be Customized.

Numeric formats in Excel provide you a lot of control over how your numbers are displayed, but they're not without flaws. There is no built-in format that allows you to display a number without the leading zero, or to display temperatures using the degree symbol, for example. You'll need to design your own numeric forms to get around these and other limitations. This can be accomplished by either altering a current format or creating one from scratch. This section goes over the formatting syntax and symbols in great detail.

The following syntax applies to all Excel numeric formats, whether built-in or customized: The four sections, which are separated by semicolons, govern how different numbers are shown. The first section specifies how a positive number should be displayed, the second section specifies how a negative number should be presented, the third section specifies how zero should be displayed, and the fourth section specifies how text should be displayed. Numbers are restricted as shown here if one or more of these sections are left out:

Number of Components

Syntax of the Format

Let's go through the basics first before moving on to some instances. To modify a numeric format, first choose the cell or range you want to format, then go through the procedures below: If the Number tab isn't already visible, go to Home, Number Format, More Number Formats (or press Ctrl+1). Select Custom from the Category drop-down menu. Select an existing format in the Type list box if you're editing it.

Your format code can be edited or entered.

Click the OK button. Excel takes you back to the worksheet where you applied the custom format. Each new format definition is saved in the Custom category in Excel. If you made changes to an existing format, the old one is kept and the new one is added to the list. Custom formats can be chosen in the same way as built-in formats are. You copy a cell holding your custom format to another worksheet to use it in that workbook

Take a look at some examples of bespoke number formats.

For each example, here's a simple explanation:

Example 1—These formats demonstrate how to use the thousands separator to reduce a huge number to a smaller, more readable number. 12300 would be displayed as 12,300.0 in a format like 0,000.0. Excel displays the value as 12.3 if you delete the three zeros between the comma and the decimal (to acquire the format 0,.0). (although it still uses the original number in calculations). In other words, you've instructed Excel to display the amount in thousands. Simply add a second thousand separators to indicate a higher number in millions.

Example 2—Use this format if you don't want any leading or trailing zeros to be seen.

Example 3—These are four-part forms in action. The first three sections specify how Excel should show positive, negative, and zero integers. If the user types text into the cell, the fourth section shows the message "Enter a number."

Example 4—The cents sign () is used after the value in this example. On your keyboard's numeric keypad, press Alt+0162 to insert the cents sign. (Using the numbers near the top of the keyboard will not work.) Table 3.8 lists some commonly used ANSI characters.

- ANSI Character Key Combinations (Table 3.8)
- Combination of Keys
- Characters in ANSI

Key Combination	ANSI Character
Alt+0162	¢
Alt+0163	£
Alt+0165	¥
Alt+0169	©
Alt+0174	®
Alt+0176	°

Example 5: The text string "Dollars" is added to the format in this example.

Example 6—An M is appended to any number in this example, which is helpful if your spreadsheet units are in megabytes.

Example 7—To represent temperatures, this example utilizes the degree symbol (°).

Case 8—In this example, the three semicolons result in no number being printed (which is useful as a basic method for hiding a sensitive value).

Example 9—In this example, you may get a number sign (#) to display in your formats by using a backslash before #. (\).

Example 10—You can see a trick for making dot trailers in this example. Keep in mind that the asterisk (*) symbol fills the cell with the character that comes after it. Adding "*." to the end of the format is all it takes to make a dot trailer.

Example 11—This example explains how to make a dot leader using a similar strategy. The first three semicolons in this example display nothing; after that, "*." runs dots from the cell's start to the text (represented by the @ sign).

Example 12—This example demonstrates a format for entering stock quotes.

Keeping Zeros Hidden

Hide extraneous zeros from worksheets to make them look less cluttered and easier to read. Excel allows you to hide zeros across the entire worksheet or just in specific cells. To conceal all zeros, go to File, Options, Excel Options dialog box, Advanced tab, and scroll down to the Display Options for this Worksheet section. Click OK after clearing the Show a Zero in Cells with Zero Value check box.

Although Google Sheets is a terrific tool for collaborating and working on spreadsheets, Excel is still the industry standard in many circles, and you'll frequently need to save your work in that format. Fortunately, Google Sheets allows you to export spreadsheets to Excel format, allowing you to work in Google Sheets while still having a fully functional Excel file.

Google Sheets Export

Once you've created your Google Sheet, you may export it to Excel by following these steps:

Step 1: Go to Google Sheets and open the sheet you wish to export.

Step 2: Open the File Menu, hover over the Download submenu to open it, and then select Microsoft Excel (.xlsx) from the drop-down menu.

Step 3: The Save File window in your browser will open.

To save your file, choose a place on your computer and a filename, then click the Save button.

Step 4: An Excel file containing a copy of your Google Sheet is now saved in the place you specified.

The file will have the extension.xlsx, and you can open it in Excel just like any other Excel file.

Summary

Example of GSheets Spreadsheet: Create a duplicate of the sample. Google Sheets is an online spreadsheet program. The Chromebook's DNA is built towards ease of use. The Chromebook user can be up and running in less than five minutes right out of the box. The Chromebook's features and functionality, by default, provide an excellent user experience without requiring significant customization. However, Google realizes that everyone is unique, and that despite having some of the top user-experience designers in the world, there is no one-size-fits-all approach to how people use technology. As a result, you have the option of customizing a number of characteristics of your Chromebook.

Printed in Great Britain
by Amazon

39744540R00088